CROW
SMARTS

CROW
SMARTS

Inside the Brain of the World's Brightest Bird

by PAMELA S. TURNER
photographs by ANDY COMINS
with art by GUIDO DE FILIPPO

HOUGHTON MIFFLIN HARCOURT
Boston   New York

To the Inkskers, who are always there for me: Carol Peterson, Nancy Humphrey Case, Keely Parrack, and Deborah Underwood. —P.S.T.

For B.L. —A.C.

All my gratitude goes to unexpected life mentors, who way too often reveal themselves in the most unforeseen disguise. —G.D.

The text type was set in Johnston ITC.
The display type was set in Freeland.

Library of Congress Cataloging-in-Publication Data

Turner, Pamela S., author.
Crow smarts / written by Pamela S. Turner.
pages cm. — (Scientists in the field)
Audience: Ages 10–14.
Audience: Grades 7 to 8.
Includes bibliographical references.

ISBN 978-0-544-41619-2

1. Crows—Behavior—Juvenile literature. 2. Animal intelligence—Juvenile literature. 3. Animal behavior—Juvenile literature. I. Title. II. Series: Scientists in the field.

QL696.P2367T87 2016

598.8'64—dc23
2015013903

Manufactured in China
SCP 10 9 8 7 6 5 4 3 2 1
4500574801

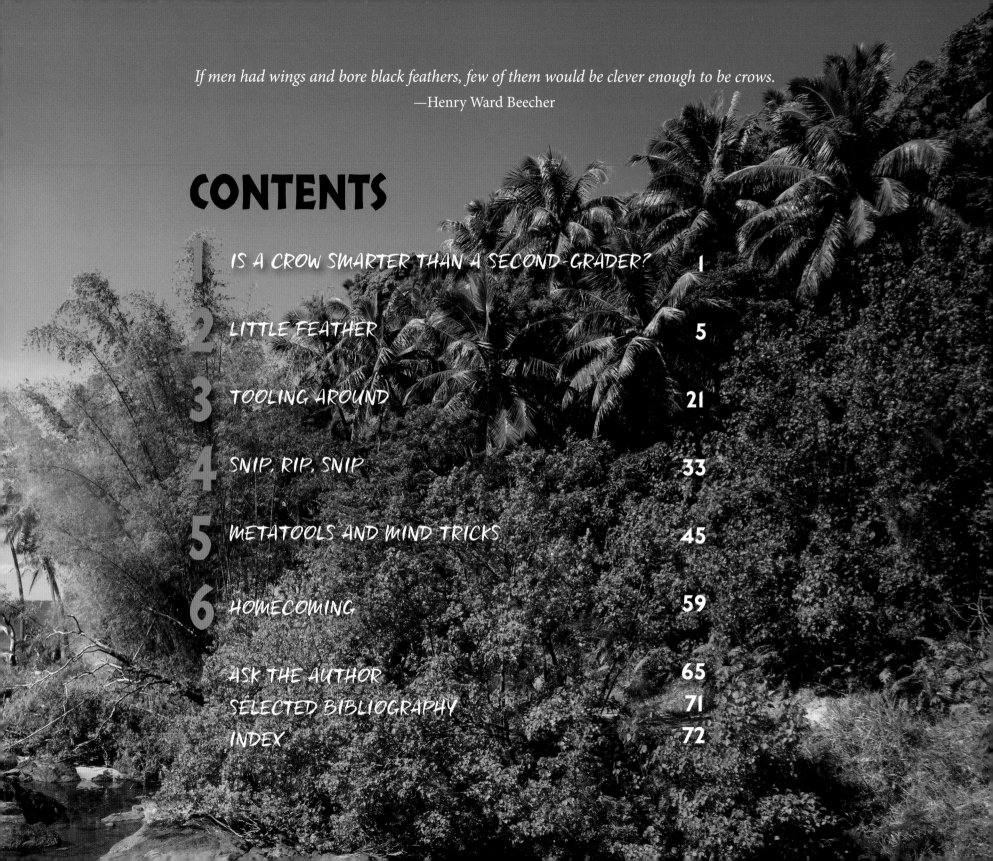

If men had wings and bore black feathers, few of them would be clever enough to be crows.
—Henry Ward Beecher

CONTENTS

A forest in New Caledonia

1 IS A CROW SMARTER THAN A SECOND-GRADER?

Munin the crow faces a test.

MUNIN HAS A PROBLEM.

A human has shooed him into a large cage that is criss-crossed with perches made from tree branches. A string hangs from one of these perches. On the other end of the string, dangling in midair, is a short stick. The short stick can't be reached by leaning down from the perch. And it's too high up to reach from the ground.

Two boxes rest on a table at the other end of the cage. Munin glides over for a look. One box is a narrow Plexiglas rectangle open at one end; a small juicy piece of beef is visible inside. Unfortunately, that fiendish human has placed the treat beyond the reach of Munin's bill.

The other box is wooden, with slats on one side, like a miniature jailhouse. Inside the slatted box—again, out of reach!—lies a long stick.

What can Munin do to get the treat? Think fast; Munin has to. If he can't solve the problem within a few minutes, the test is over.

Munin gazes at the short stick.

Now imagine a different problem. You're shown a small treat-filled bucket inside a narrow tube, and the tube can't be moved. The bucket is at the bottom of the tube, and the handle of the bucket is out of reach of your fingers (or a crow's bill). You're given a length of wire. Quick! What's the solution?

Here's another test: A treat floats in water at the bottom of a tube, again out of reach. But there are some stones nearby. What's the answer? How do you get the treat?

The solutions that crows such as Munin come up with might surprise you. Crows may not have fingers, but they do have nimble bills and feet. Crows also have another important quality, one that is rare and special. It's the ability to understand the world around them. The ability to reason, to remember, to keep a goal in mind. The ability to imagine and invent. The ability to create.

We call this quality "intelligence."

Welcome to New Caledonia, where the forests are lush and the crows are geniuses.

Munin can't reach the long stick in the back of the wooden box, but he needs it to reach the chunk of meat in the Plexiglas box.

3

Little Feather (on left) is a lucky bird. Only about one-fifth of crow chicks survive their perilous first few months. Some are victims of high winds that blow youngsters out of their nests. Others are killed by goshawks.

2 LITTLE FEATHER

Little Feather spots a grub.

WAAAH . . . WAAAH . . . WAAAH . . .

The begging call of a juvenile New Caledonian crow gets louder as the bird moves closer. A moment later, two sleek, shiny crows land on the log in front of us. We watch them through slits in a camouflaged tent.

It's easy to identify the youngster, who never stops *waaah*-ing. One small plume on its shoulder is tweaked upward like a fluffy shoulder pad. The other crow must be Little Feather's mom or dad. It's hard to imagine anyone else putting up with this much whining.

Four little feet *tap-tap-tap* across the log. Earlier that day we drilled holes in the crumbling wood and filled them with pleasingly plump beetle larvae. The crows twist their glossy heads to peek inside. I imagine them thinking, *Eureka! It's a mother lode of grub steaks!*

Little Feather stakes out a position at the end of the log. *Waaah . . . waaah . . .*

The adult bird hops to the ground, picks up a dried leaf stem, and jumps back up onto the log. Holding the stem in its bill, it probes the hole with swift, sharp jabs. After a few seconds it drops the leaf-stem tool and sticks its bill into the hole. Little Feather picks up the tool as if to give it a go, but the adult snatches it back, immediately flipping it around. Clearly it has a strong opinion about which end of the stem is the poking end.

Yet Little Feather's parent still seems dissatisfied. It discards the stem and hops off in search of a better tool. Luckily, the forest floor is covered in sticks, twigs, and dry stems. It's a crow Home Depot.

The adult returns with a different (new and improved?) leaf stem. Jab–jab–jab–jab. All of this jabbing isn't intended to stab the grub, as you might expect. Instead the crow is using the tip of its tool to irritate the grub inside the hole. If the crow can rouse the grub's fighting spirit . . . and get the tip of the tool between the grub's stubby jaws . . .

Little Feather's only contribution is a steady stream of *waaah . . . waaah . . . waaah . . .*

After four minutes of delicate work, the grub clamps onto the crow's tool like a bulldog. Little Feather's parent hauls out its catch. It's big and lumpy: the Jabba the Hutt of grubs!

The adult crow snatches its prize and zooms into a nearby tree. *Waaah . . . waaah . . . waaah . . .* wails Little Feather, winging away in desperate pursuit. *Waaah . . . waaah . . . waaah . . .* The young crow has perfected a technique known by children everywhere: just keep whining until Mom or Dad finally cracks.

Sure enough, a moment later we hear the cartoonish *glug-glug-glug* that fledgling crows make when they're being fed. Little Feather has scored!

Afterward the forest settles into a comfortable naptime quiet. The hoot of a wild pigeon drifts from a distant hillside; a soft breeze shushes through the treetops.

Waaah . . . waaah . . . waaah . . . waaah . . .

Yes, it's Little Feather, acting as if he hasn't eaten since the last ice age, instead of only two minutes ago.

⋀ When Little Feather's parent drops its tool, Little Feather picks it up and the adult bird takes it back. As they watch Mom or Dad, young crows are probably learning essential survival skills.

∧ Success! When New Caledonian crows find a grub and try to extract it with a tool, they get a meal about 70 percent of the time.

∧ We cut away the wood to show how an irritated grub latches on to a leaf stem.

Poor underfed Little Feather.

7

WILD CROWS USING TOOLS—it's a startling notion. In some ways this tool use is a new discovery, and in some ways it isn't.

In 1882 a scientist wrote a report about New Caledonian birds. He claimed that the island's crows carry candlenuts "to a considerable altitude, and then drop them on a stone or hard root to crack them." In 1928 a French travel book casually mentioned New Caledonian crows using stick tools to pull grubs from dead wood. Neither of these reports attracted attention.

In those days scientists believed that only humans had the intelligence to make and use tools. Tool use made us special. Louis Leakey, a famous scientist who studied early human ancestors, wrote that toolmaking was the "step which lifted 'near-man' from the purely animal level to that of human status."

Louis Leakey hoped that the study of living apes might help scientists understand humanity's apelike ancestors. He encouraged an animal-loving young woman to begin the first-ever study of wild chimpanzees. Her name was Jane Goodall.

Jane set up a study site in Tanzania, a country in East Africa. On a November morning in 1960 Jane saw a chimp she had named David Greybeard pick at a piece of straw, poke it into a termite mound, and pull it out covered in termites. The chimpanzee lifted the straw to his mouth and nibbled off the insects.

An ape making a tool! Jane immediately sent a telegram to Louis Leakey. He responded, "Now we must redefine 'man,' redefine 'tool,' or accept chimpanzees as humans."

Chimpanzees use a variety of tools, including grass stems, sticks, and stones. Like New Caledonian crows, they seem to learn by watching others.

This American alligator with a mouthful of snowy egret used a stick balanced on its snout as "bait." Alligators sometimes carry sticks on their snouts during the time of year when wading birds are looking for material to build nests.

After Jane's discovery, other scientists found evidence of tool use in a wide variety of species. Some species of ants use tiny pieces of leaf, wood, and soil to carry soft foods such as honey or fruit pulp. Some species of crabs pull small stinging anemones off rocks and wave the anemones in their claws to fend off predators. Some alligators, during nest-making season, balance sticks on their snouts as "bait"; when a heron or an egret flies down to pick up the stick, the bird becomes lunch. (You have to admire that level of sneakiness.) Capuchin monkeys use stones to dig out plant roots and crack nuts. A group of bottle-nose dolphins in Western Australia use sea sponges to protect their rostrums (beaks) as they search through seafloor rubble for bottom-dwelling fish.

These discoveries have raised important questions: What exactly is a tool? Is tool use really a sign of intelligence?

Scientists now define "tool behavior" as the use of an unattached object to manipulate something else. Construction projects such as nest building and web spinning don't qualify. A beaver using a branch to make a dam isn't using a tool. But if you see a beaver firing up a chain saw to cut a branch, yes, that's tool use. Please take a video.

In Shark Bay, Australia, a bottlenose dolphin brings its tool—a basket sponge—to the surface. Only a small group of dolphins use sponges as tools, even though sponges are common in bottlenose dolphin habitats. "Sponging" seems to be a cultural practice.

So, does tool use always equal intelligence? Scientists think that some tool behaviors are "programmed" while others are "flexible." Programmed tool use—the kind seen in ants and crabs—doesn't vary from individual to individual and shows up in every member of the species. It's instinctive. But flexible tool use is different. Not every member of the species uses a tool, and individuals vary in how and when they use their tools. (If you're wondering about those sneaky alligators, scientists debate whether the alligator's behavior is truly tool use since the alligator isn't *holding* the stick; it's also debatable whether the behavior is instinctive or not. Regardless, scientists are beginning to realize that alligators are far smarter than anyone thought.)

Flexible tool use by wild animals is rare. So far it has been observed in only a few species, including capuchin monkeys, elephants, chimpanzees, bottlenose dolphins, and New Caledonian crows. What's even rarer is the ability not just to *use* a tool, but to *make* a tool. In this category the New Caledonian crow may shine brighter than all other nonhuman animals—including Jane Goodall's famous chimpanzees.

≪ The discarded shells of candlenuts broken open by the crows.

A FEW DAYS BEFORE, Gavin had brought the photographer Andy Comins and me to a New Caledonian forest to show us crow tool use in action. We drove past Sarraméa, a village with a tidy tin-roofed school and a small roadside park. When the road dead-ended, we hiked uphill to a grove of candlenut trees.

Candlenut trees offer a food bonanza for New Caledonian crows. "The trees provide grubs and nuts all year round," Gavin explained. "Both are a bit tricky to get, but if you can figure it out, you eat well."

Gavin showed us a fork in a candlenut tree branch. A large rock directly below the fork was littered with broken shells—candlenut shells and the shells of a snail that has been introduced to New Caledonia by humans. "Instead of just randomly dropping the nut or snail somewhere on the rock to crack it, the crows set it in the fork and push it off," explained Gavin as he pointed upward. "The crows are aiming their drop. It's not tool use, but it shows how flexible their behavior is." By aiming their drop, the crows make sure the nut or snail hits the rock rather than landing in the softer dirt nearby.

I smashed a candlenut with a rock (classic tool use!) and nibbled some of the meat. "Ugh—it tastes like dirt—" I sputtered.

"Try this one," offered Gavin, who is far too polite to point out that I just ate a rotten candlenut.

Fresh candlenuts taste like a cross between macadamia nuts and coconut. I cracked open another.

"Yes, well, I wouldn't eat too much," Gavin said. "It's a laxative."

↑ A crow carries a candlenut into a tree and uses a forked branch to aim its drop.

Which is a nice way of saying *You might spend the rest of the day huddled in a bathroom.* Or huddled in the shrubbery.

Gavin selected a small clearing among the candlenut trees and showed us how to set up a feeding station. Feeding stations bring the crows in close for observation. We opened our pop-up blind and dragged a fallen log in front. Gavin drilled deep, narrow holes across the top of the log and on one end. Next we needed grubs to stuff inside.

We found a Goliath-size candlenut log rotting nearby.

Between swings with a crowbar, Gavin explained how the crows find grubs in dead wood: "They hear the larvae munching away down inside. Then they get a tool and poke in the holes and crevices."

Once split, the rotten wood revealed snug tunnels stuffed with grubs. We pulled them out one by one and put them in a plastic box. We needed plenty of crow bait for our days of crow observation. Once the crows become accustomed to the feeding station, Gavin will try to capture a few of the birds. He has designed and built a new kind of crow–catching net that he hopes to test.

Gavin is a quiet, versatile, competent man, the sort of person who could survive in the wilderness with just a few tools. Sort of like the crows he studies.

As a boy growing up on a farm in New Zealand, he spent a lot of time outdoors. In his twenties he traveled to Africa to see the wildlife. He returned home to work on the family farm but nursed a dream: he wanted to become a wildlife conservationist.

Gavin didn't start college until age thirty. In 1993, while doing research for his Ph.D. in ecology, he made a stunning discovery about New Caledonian crows. It happened by accident.

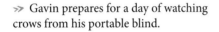
≫ Gavin prepares for a day of watching crows from his portable blind.

⋏ Splitting apart dead candlenut wood reveals the larvae of long-horned beetles. Gavin stores the juicy "crow bait" in a fishing tackle box.

Wild crows are very wary and hard to follow in a dense forest. A feeding station such as this one allows scientists to observe the crows close up.

"I wasn't studying crows at all," Gavin explained. "I was studying kagu."

The kagu is a rare bird found only in New Caledonia. Gavin wanted to find out how many were left. Since the near-flightless kagu (it glides, but cannot fly) is hard to spot in a dense forest, Gavin counted them by recording the number of calls they made. An area with more kagu calls was probably an area with a larger population of kagus. As he hiked through the underbrush with his tape recorder, he often glimpsed crows.

In June 1992 he was working near Monts Dzumac in the

13

southern part of New Caledonia. Gavin spotted a crow poking a stick in a hole, clearly trying to fish something out. Although in 1972 and 1980 scientists had published brief accounts of New Caledonian crows using sticks as tools, the behavior wasn't well known in the scientific community. Gavin was fascinated. Here were crows using tools, just like Jane Goodall's famous chimpanzees!

From that moment on, Gavin paid special attention to the crows. On February 9, 1993, he wrote in his field notes:

> One crow up in a tree with a pandanus [a plant] tool in its bill . . . After several minutes another crow arrived, also with a stick tool that had a hook at one end. It probed a horizontal branch—I could not see the probe site. Both birds then put

≪ "Crows have a lot of personality," says Gavin. "I like that they live in family groups and look after each other. They seem a lot like us."

down their tools next to themselves. I clapped and both crows flew off. The second bird picked up its tool though. I retrieved the first crow's pandanus tool that was lodged between a vine and a branch. It had black dirt on the probing end.

Gavin tried to collect as many crow tools as possible. Often the crows objected to donating their tools to science. After being shooed away from their tools, the crows sometimes followed Gavin, squawking indignantly.

The variety of the tools he collected showed the crows' true inventiveness. Some were straight sticks. Some tools were twigs that had been carefully snipped and whittled on one end to create a hook. Others were made from strips torn from the long, stiff barb-edged leaves of the pandanus plant. Yet the pandanus tools were not random rips. Some were wide and some were narrow, and some were carefully torn in a stair-step fashion. The stepped tools were designed so that one end was thicker and stiffer (the better to hold in the crow's bill) while the other was thinner and more flexible (the better to poke into crevices). And all the stepped tools were oriented so that the barbs that ran along the edge of the pandanus leaf pointed upward (the better to snag a worm or a spider).

To observe New Caledonian crows *using* tools was interesting enough. But to discover that the crows were creating a utility belt's worth of *manufactured* tools—that was truly stunning.

How did crows become so smart?

≫ The New Caledonian crow "tool chest" contains (top to bottom) stepped pandanus tools, narrow pandanus tools, wide pandanus tools, hooked sticks, and more-or-less straight sticks. New Caledonian crows are the only animals besides humans that make hooked tools. The hook on the stick tool was shaped by a crow; the hooks on the pandanus leaf tools are natural barbs on the leaf edge.

 WE WATCH THE LOG FROM THE BLIND. A few hours later Little Feather returns, along with a parent. The youngster peers into the holes we previously filled with grubs.

Waaah . . . waaah . . .

Little Feather picks up a leaf stem left behind by one of the adults. Somehow, the juvenile manages to continue *waaah*-ing even with a stem in its mouth. Jab, move to a different hole, jab, jab, move, jab again, all the time moving down the log toward the adult bird, as if to say, *Look, I'm trying, but it's not working. Help!*

After exactly seventeen seconds of effort Little Feather drops the leaf stem. The adult retrieves it and, as if it were holding a jackhammer, starts jabbing a hole. Little Feather moves over to eye the action and continues begging. Just in case Mom or Dad didn't hear the first twenty *waaah*s.

New Caledonian crows such as Little Feather grow up in small, stable, caring families. Mom and Dad mate for life. They build their nest high in a tree, and Mom lays two or three bluish, brown-speckled eggs. Mom incubates the eggs while Dad flies in all the meals. Little Feather left the nest—possibly with a brother or sister—about one month after hatching. In most bird species, a chick is on its own soon after leaving the nest. But a young New Caledonian crow like Little Feather will probably remain glued to Mom and Dad for a year (until the next breeding season), and perhaps even longer. Tool use seems to demand a long apprenticeship.

ʌ Learning to fish for grubs with a stick is like learning to write your name. It requires practice and persistence.

A beetle larva (left) spends about two years eating through wood before gradually transforming into a beetle pupa (right) and finally into an adult beetle.

Almost there! Gavin once watched a crow spend forty-five minutes teasing out a grub. The effort is worth the reward, however. Three average-size grubs provide a crow's daily energy needs.

Little Feather is certainly paying close attention to its parent's grub-fishing efforts. The grub's head appears . . . and falls back down. Oops. The adult crow stares at Little Feather for a moment before resuming the jab-jab-jab.

The adult crow pauses. It pulls out the leaf-stem tool, looks around, probes the hole, then stops again. It deliberately flips its tool and tries the other end. Jab-jab-jab. Every time Little Feather's parent picks up the leaf stem, it holds the tool angled along the same side of its head. The left side.

By catching and banding dozens of crows and watching how individual crows use their tools, Gavin and his colleagues discovered that New Caledonian crows have what we would call "handedness." (Since crows don't have hands, the scientific term is "laterality.") We write using either our right hand or our left; a New Caledonian crow holds its tool along either the right or the left side of its head.

Little Feather's left-handed parent persists. Again and again the grub comes up and slides back. Slippery little sucker! Finally, enough grub emerges; Little Feather pounces. Apparently the adult wasn't planning to give away its hard-earned lunch, because it lunges toward Little Feather. Too late! Little Feather guzzles the grub: *Glub-glub-glub.*

Shortly followed by (surely you saw this coming!) . . . *waaah . . . waaah . . . waaah . . .*

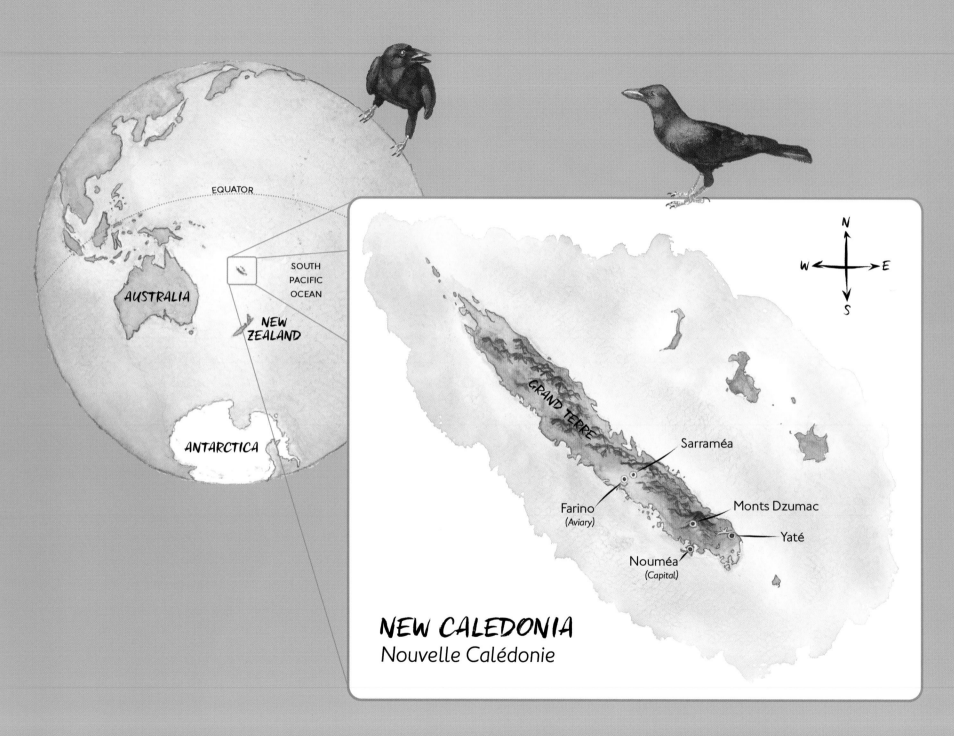

EQUATOR

AUSTRALIA

NEW ZEALAND

SOUTH PACIFIC OCEAN

ANTARCTICA

N
W E
S

GRAND TERRE

Sarraméa

Farino
(Aviary)

Monts Dzumac

Yaté

Nouméa
(Capital)

NEW CALEDONIA
Nouvelle Calédonie

NEW CALEDONIA

Man made brushfires are a major cause of forest loss in New Caledonia.

New Caledonia is a remote group of islands in the South Pacific. The Kanak people have lived there for at least 2,800 years. The English explorer Captain James Cook visited in 1174, and in 1853 France claimed the islands as a colony. New Caledonia is now a French Overseas Territory, and its 250,000 residents are French citizens. Most people live on the main island, Grande Terre, which is larger than the U.S. state of Connecticut but smaller than New Jersey. Lush mountains run along the island's spine; lowland scrub fringes the coasts.

Among the world's tropical islands, New Caledonia is one of the richest in terms of biodiversity (the number and uniqueness of different species). Of the 3,425 plants on the island, 2,541 (74 percent) are found nowhere else. Some New Caledonia trees are the last relatives of species that covered the world 65 million years ago, during the time of the dinosaurs.

New Caledonia also has many unique reptiles; of the 71 reptile species found in New Caledonia, 62 (87 percent) live only there. And among its 175 bird species, 21 are unique. If you want to see a New Caledonian crow, you'll have to visit these islands.

The wonders extend offshore. The fringing reefs of New Caledonia are home to 457 species of coral and 1,695 species of reef fish. (In comparison, the *entire* Caribbean Sea has only about 60 coral species and 600 species of reef fish.)

Unfortunately, this biodiversity is under threat. Although it has relatively few people, New Caledonia lost 29 percent of its forests between 1989 and 2009. Most of the forest loss has been caused by brushfires. Hunters set brushfires because rusa deer and wild pigs are attracted to the new plants that spring up on newly burned land, and can then be hunted more easily. Rusa deer and wild pigs are nonnative species that damage the New Caledonian ecosystem and threaten its native plants and animals. Conservationists are trying to find new ways to control both brushfires and invasive species.

New Caledonian crows create tools from a variety of materials: twigs, leaf stems, dry grass, thorny vines, and pandanus leaves. Occasionally, in captivity, they will use discarded cardboard or their own molted feathers.

3 TOOLING AROUND

YOU MIGHT THINK THAT INTELLIGENCE IS A BIG ADVANTAGE. After all, we humans have big brains and we're super successful (if we define success as a large population). So why hasn't evolution produced thousands of super-smart species?

Evolution by natural selection means that in every generation, individuals vary. The individuals with qualities best suited to their environment survive and reproduce; they leave behind more offspring than individuals poorly suited to their environment. Eventually the qualities that help a species survive spread throughout the population.

It seems as if a big, complex brain should always be a helpful quality. Shouldn't the smarter individuals survive? Shouldn't the dumb ones be killed off? Life has been evolving on Earth for 3.5 billion years. Why don't we see big-brained sharks negotiating peace treaties with surfers? Where are the squirrels with over-size heads competing on *Jeopardy!*?

As it turns out, big brains usually aren't necessary. Jellyfish do their thing without any brain at all. Sharks are small-brained yet have survived for hundreds of millions of years. If it isn't broken, there's no need to fix it.

It's not easy for a big brain to evolve, because big brains are quite costly. Brain tissue eats up more energy than other body tissues, just as a race car burns more fuel than a lawnmower. A big brain requires a payoff that makes up for the extra energy it consumes.

In addition to needing lots of fuel, brain size is limited in other ways, depending on how an animal lives and reproduces. If a high percentage of a bird's body weight is in its head, the aerodynamics of flight don't work. (That's also why birds don't have teeth—teeth are heavy and would overweight the head.) Human bodies have limits too. A baby's skull (and therefore the brain inside)

⋎ Lefty and Little Feather eye the feeding station from a nearby branch. Crows sometimes carry a favorite tool from place to place . . . and sometimes stash their tool under their foot while eating so they don't lose it.

can't get too large, because the baby's head must fit through its mother's pelvis during birth.

Big brains are rare. Mammals that have evolved big, complex brains are primates (monkeys and great apes), cetaceans (whales and dolphins), and elephants. Among birds, those with the biggest brains for their body size are parrots and corvids (a group that includes crows and ravens).

If we go back 280 million years, to the last common ancestor of mammals and birds, we find a reptilian creature that was most definitely lacking in the smarts department. From this common starting point the mammals evolved along one line and the birds evolved along another. Yet some mammal and bird species ended up with big, complex brains. When different species take different paths and end up at a similar point, scientists call it "convergent evolution."

Oddly enough, even though their bodies and brain structures are very different, crows and humans may have gone down the path leading to more complex brains at about the same time, and for similar reasons.

« The crow version of a human behavior often seen in toy stores.

MEANWHILE, BACK AT THE LOG . . .
Little Feather and the left-handed adult crow are after more grubs. Lefty picks up a leaf stem and probes a hole briefly before flipping the tool around to try the other end. Every movement is nimble and precise.

Little Feather leaps over Lefty's head in a single bound. *Waaah . . . waaah . . .* The youngster fluffs its feathers and shakes its wings in a classic baby-bird-begging pose. Just in case Lefty is deaf.

After a few moments the youngster seems to realize that some self-help might be in order. Little Feather jumps down and returns with a leaf stem but drops it almost immediately. The juvenile walks over to stare into Lefty's hole with a beady black eye.

Lefty casts aside its leaf stem and hops to the ground to search for something better. Little Feather seems at a loss. By now, however, Lefty has scored a new and improved leaf stem, and sets to work. The adult crow snaps off the end of the leaf stem, flips it around, probes, and flips it again. But the grub in the hole isn't grabbing the stem. Little Feather continues to urge Lefty along: *Waaah . . . waaah . . . waaah . . .*

New Caledonian crows such as Lefty and Little Feather look similar to other crow species, but their bills are straighter. Their eyes are bigger and more forward-pointing, giving them better binocular vision. ("Binocular" means "two eyes together." Each eye has a certain field of vision that it can see; when the fields of vision of the two eyes overlap, that is binocular vision. Binocular

⋏ Little Feather tries grub fishing.

≪ New Caledonian crows have a straight bill that resembles needle-nose pliers. ≫

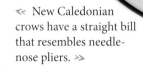

≫ Most other crow species (such as this American crow) have bills that curve slightly downward.

vision gives better depth perception.) Scientists think these differences may have evolved as a result of tool use.

It might have happened this way: We know that individual New Caledonian crows (like individuals of every species) vary from one another. Some have bills that are slightly straighter; some have eyes that are larger or smaller, or set slightly more toward the front or toward the sides. Those crows with slightly straighter bills and slightly larger, more forward-set eyes probably had an easier time using tools. A straighter bill allows the crow to hold a tool more firmly. Larger eyes oriented more to the front give the bird a better view of the tip of a stick held in the bird's bill. So those birds with straighter bills and larger, more forward-pointing eyes were probably better tool users. They ate better and raised more offspring, out-competing other crows;

Both humans and New Caledonian crows are able to grip their tools firmly and guide them accurately.

they were better adapted to their environment. Over many generations, the straighter bills and forward-oriented eyes spread through the crow population on New Caledonia.

Yes, crows shape tools. But tools may also shape crows.

Unfortunately, the chosen tool doesn't always work well. Lefty drops the leaf stem it was using and jumps to the ground again, casting about like a mechanic in search of the right wrench. Little Feather picks up Lefty's old tool and probes a hole. This time Little Feather is definitely looking before poking and seems to be putting in a bit more thought and effort. Is Little Feather "left-handed" or "right-handed"? Since the youngster always holds the very end of the stick in its bill, we can't tell.

Lefty returns with a Y-shaped twig. An interesting choice. Shaping will be needed to fit the twig into the hole. The crow snaps off one end of the Y and then snaps off a small straight length of stick. With one probe Lefty recognizes that the stick is too short and discards it. Little Feather, meanwhile, is moving along the log: peek in hole, jab-jab, peek in hole, *waaah . . . waaah . . .* The youngster is trying.

After once again tool shopping on the forest floor, Lefty returns with a very twiggy twig. Even more shaping will be necessary. Snip, snap: the crow prunes like an opinionated gardener. The result is a long, slightly curved stick tool.

Waak. Waak.

Somewhere in the distance another crow is making a "contact call": the crow equivalent of *Hey, I'm over here!* Lefty, still holding the new stick tool, gives a single *waak* in response. Crow

⋀ New Caledonian crows make hooked tools by snipping and shaping a forked branch.

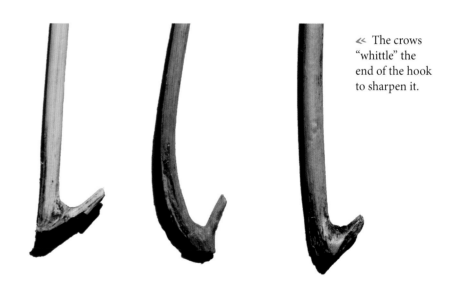

« The crows "whittle" the end of the hook to sharpen it.

25

families stay in close contact even when they can't see each other. If a crow is alarmed, the *waak* calls will be sharper and spaced closer together, depending on the threat level. Humans usually rate a code yellow. A hawk is code red: *WAAK! WAAK! WAAK! WAAK!*

Waaah . . . waaah . . . waaah . . . whines Little Feather. At least everyone always knows where the baby of the family is.

Little Feather sets the tool aside to watch Lefty. After a few probes, the adult crow takes out the stick tool and makes another adjustment. Snip. This leaves a sharper bend at the tip end. Not quite a hook, but getting there. Lefty draws a small bite of something out of the hole and pecks it off the stick. It seems that the delicate "poke until the grub grabs the end of the stick" technique has been abandoned in favor of a cruder "skewer the stupid thing" method. Little Feather peers keenly into the hole, wings fluffed for another bout of begging.

Lefty pulls out another small bit. It must be pretty grubby down there.

Jabbing harder than ever, Lefty manages to lever the larva out with the hooked end of the tool. The adult bird immediately swivels away from Little Feather and flies off with a plump grub dangling from its bill. Little Feather pursues, *waaah*ing pitifully.

Extracting two big grubs—this one and the one snatched away earlier by Little Feather—has taken Lefty about fourteen minutes of determined effort. For most of that time, Little Feather either watched intently or fiddled with a tool in apparent imitation of its parent. You might say that Little Feather is being homeschooled.

SCIENTISTS HAVE NOTICED THAT ALL THE SMARTER species (such as humans, chimps, dolphins, and crows) live in groups. What does social living have to do with intelligence?

In all of these species, group living probably started off as a defense against predators. A leopard in the bush, a shark in the depths, or a hawk in the sky is more likely to be spotted if many pairs of eyes are on the lookout. And a predator sure to attack a lone individual might hesitate to attack a large group, especially if the members of the group will band together to fight off the predator.

Once animals create a community for protection, other possibilities open up. Members of the group can cooperate in finding and sharing food. They may also compete for the most attractive mate. Regardless of whether you are cooperating or competing, it's an advantage if you can recognize, remember, negotiate with, and communicate with others in your group. And that requires brainpower.

Scientists think that the intense social lives of humans, chimps, dolphins, and crows may have driven the evolution of their big, complex brains. (This idea is called the social intelligence hypothesis. A hypothesis is a proposed explanation.) The challenges of finding food are probably also linked to the evolution of intelligence. Some scientists think that the species that eat a wide variety of foods—and have to work hard to get at those foods—are more likely to evolve bigger brains. (This idea

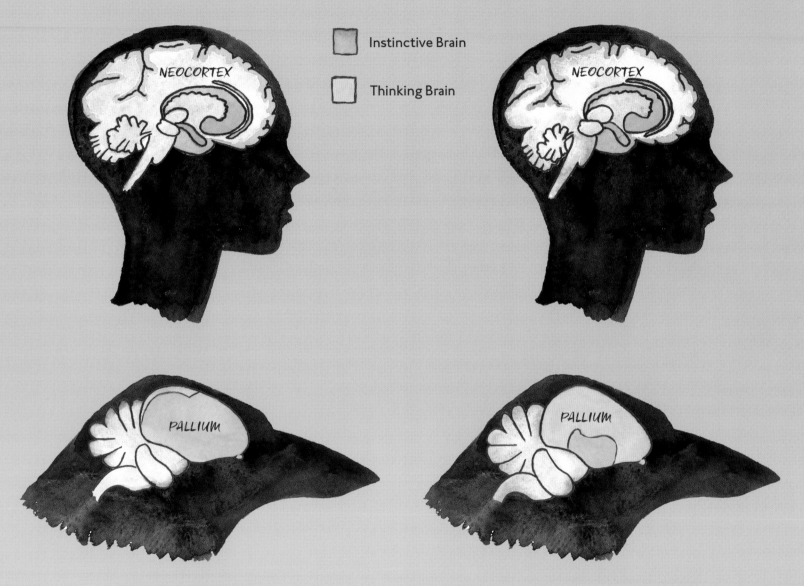

WHAT WE USED TO THINK

WHAT WE KNOW NOW

Instinctive Brain

Thinking Brain

NEOCORTEX

NEOCORTEX

PALLIUM

PALLIUM

In mammals, complex thought is formed in the neocortex, the wrinkly surface of the brain. Birds don't have a neocortex, so scientists assumed that birds don't really think, and rely mostly on instinct. But there's more than one way to build a brain. Scientists now know that a different part of a bird's brain (the pallium) acts like a mammal's neocortex. Rather than being primitive, birds' brains are simply wired differently.

Candlenut trees provide a rich food source for crows, but the nuts are hard to crack and the grubs are difficult to extract from the dead wood.

is the technical intelligence hypothesis.) Social intelligence and technical intelligence may work together to produce a brain as sharp and as versatile as a Swiss Army knife.

Consider humans and crows. The earliest human ancestors and the earliest crow species both appeared some five to ten million years ago. During that period there was a lot of climate change. Ice ages waxed and waned. Food available at a certain place during a certain season might suddenly disappear, or a water source might dry up. Forests became grassland; grassland flipped to scrubland; scrubland greened and turned back to forest. The challenge was stark and simple: Adapt or die.

This seesaw environment probably drove the evolution of intelligence in both humans and crows. Social living became even more important. We alerted others in our group when we found food, and they returned the favor. Brains already made complex by the demands of social life could be turned toward other problems, such as how to find and exploit new food sources. Human ancestors and crow ancestors were flexible and creative foragers; our specialty was not specializing. Seeds, fruit, insect larvae, lion leftovers, whatever. We were not picky eaters.

These qualities helped humans and crows survive, succeed, and spread. Since then we've both gone global, like Starbucks and McDonald's.

Sure, humans are unique. We've surged ahead of all other species and have used our brains to transform the world. We build such things as cars, roads, and pedestrian crossings. Crows don't. But crows still excel at exploiting new environments and new food sources. In Japan, the local crows set walnuts down at intersections so passing cars will drive over the shells and crack them open. When the pedestrian light turns on, the crows saunter out to eat the nuts.

Some people compliment crows by calling them "feathered apes." Maybe in their kinder moments the birds think of us as "grounded crows."

^ Sudden success!

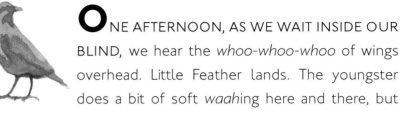

ONE AFTERNOON, AS WE WAIT INSIDE OUR BLIND, we hear the *whoo-whoo-whoo* of wings overhead. Little Feather lands. The youngster does a bit of soft *waah*ing here and there, but halfheartedly, as if aware there's no parent standing by.

Little Feather peeks into a hole. A grub! The youngster tries to cram its entire head inside, even though the food is out of reach—a rookie mistake. Successful tool use requires self-control. Little Feather must squelch this natural urge to go straight for the food.

Wait, Little Feather. Think!

A few tools left behind by adult crows teeter atop the log. Little Feather struts down the log to fetch one. Poke-poke-poke. The youngster switches stance and probes at an angle. Little Feather seems to be trying to get the stem under the grub and lift it out, the same technique Lefty used with the second grub. Because this hole is wide at the top, Little Feather has room to angle the tool without breaking it. This just might work.

Jab-jab-jab. The tool flips up, and a big white whale of a grub somersaults over Little Feather's head. Startled, the youngster hops straight into the air. Just as quickly Little Feather recovers, pounces, and gargles the grub: *Glub-glub-glub.*

A moment later the young crow flies off with a (possibly triumphant) *Waak! Waak!*

"Yeah, that's the thing about juveniles," Gavin says. "They play dumb, but when their parent goes off, they do pretty well by themselves."

ODE TO EYEBALL EATING

There are lovely traditional phrases that refer to groups of birds, such as "an exaltation of larks," "a charm of finches," and "a parliament of owls." But a group of crows is called "a murder of crows."

Crows are often considered evil, as if they were Sith Lords with wings. After all, crows are as dark as night, a hue that reminds people of their fears. Crows call to one another in harsh voices. They are notorious for feasting on farmers' corn. Crows prey on the nestlings of adorable birds, such as robins and sparrows. And perhaps worst of all, crows peck the eyeballs of dead things.

Here's the real story: Black feathers are the hardiest feathers because they have the most melanin (a natural pigment that also strengthens). Whatever you think of the voices of crows, scientists classify them as members of the songbird family. Yes, that's right: crows are songsters. Just think of them as heavy metal guitarists rather than classical violinists.

Crows do eat farmers' corn. Guilty as charged. More to the point, however, crows in cornfields are mostly after bugs, and their usefulness in ridding cornfields of pests far outweighs the corn they eat.

The belief that crows eat lots of baby birds is a myth. When scientists in North America aimed cameras at nests, they discovered that crows were responsible for

↑ A murder of squirrels.

only 1 percent of attacks. The most common nest predators were snakes (34 percent of attacks), followed by—believe it or not—squirrels and chipmunks (16 percent of attacks). Doesn't that make you wonder what's *really* stuffed into those cute cheeks?

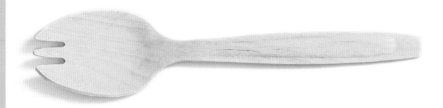

↑ The mighty spork. It's the crow's bill of eating utensils.

And finally, the eyeball thing. Crows are omnivores, which means they eat all sorts of things. Many other birds specialize in one kind of food. A hawk has a knifelike bill for cutting flesh; a flamingo has a scooplike bill for filtering snails and plants out of the water. The crow has a general-purpose bill. It isn't great at anything but handles most foods fairly well. It's the spork of bird bills.

Imagine you're a crow perched atop a road-killed raccoon. Your fledgling daughter is begging in desperate hunger. At any moment a bigger scavenger might show up: a coyote, or a turkey vulture, or a guy driving an Animal Control truck. Your bill isn't strong enough to tear through the raccoon's hide. So what do you do?

You go for the eyeball.

Sure, it's icky. But it's nutritious and easy to grab. If it makes you feel any better, that eyeball-eating crow would probably rather be gulping muscle or guts. And if you find *that* disgusting, you probably don't want to know what goes into hot dogs.

↑ The New Caledonian crow is part of the corvid family. Corvids include crows, ravens, magpies, and jays: a total of about 120 species. Of those 120 corvid species, about 40 are crows. Crows are found almost everywhere except South America, the Arctic, and the Antarctic.

CARNIVORE: An animal that eats other animals.

HERBIVORE: An animal that eats plants.

OMNIVORE: An animal that eats animals and plants.

INSECTIVORE: An animal that eats insects.

FRUGIVORE: An animal that eats fruit.

PIZZA-VORE: Just checking to see if you're still awake.

The highlands above Sarrameá, with Monts Dzumac in the distance.

4 SNIP, RIP, SNIP

<< These stepped pandanus tools were made by wild New Caledonian crows. To make a stepped pandanus tool, a crow must learn rules about how and where to tear the pandanus leaf.

∨ The hand ax is one of the earliest human tools. Hand axes have a sharp edge for cutting and a rounded edge for holding. To make a hand ax, a person must learn rules about how to use one stone to flake off bits of rock from another stone.

AFTER THREE DAYS HUDDLED IN THE BLIND, watching Little Feather, Lefty, and the rest of the local crow crowd, we take a hike farther into the hills. Away from candlenut trees and into the land of pandanus. Along the way, we startle a crow. *Waak! Waak! Waak!* it calls before winging away.

As we walk, I ask Gavin what he thinks is the most interesting question about New Caledonian crows.

"Have the crows improved their tools over time?" Gavin says. "That's the big question. We humans can have an innovation. We can hold on to it, and then future generations can improve on the idea. Have New Caledonian crows done that? That's why the pandanus tools are so interesting."

The earliest human tools were probably sticks, which were used to dig up roots, and stones, which were used to crack nuts or cut up animal carcasses. Over time, our tool kit improved and expanded. We invented bows and arrows, spears, knives, and axes . . . and eventually everything from x-ray machines to nuclear weapons. We passed along what we learned and built things based on earlier discoveries and technologies. This is called cumulative cultural evolution. Most scientists think that cumulative cultural evolution is unique to humans.

33

Gavin leads us to a sunlit plateau. From here, standing on the spine of the island, we can see both the east and west coasts. Gavin points to a cone of green rising in the south. "That's where I was, studying the kagu, when I first saw the crows using tools," he says.

You might wonder why New Caledonia is the only place where wild corvids regularly use tools. After all, crows and ravens worldwide are known for intelligence, curiosity, and their habit of playing with odd objects. There's a popular Russian video of a crow using the lid of a mayonnaise jar to sled down a snowy roof. In Colorado, eight ravens were spotted "windsurfing"—clutching tree bark in their feet and angling the bark into a strong gust so they could soar, dive, and veer without flapping their wings. During a football game at the University of Washington, thousands of spectators watched a flock of fifty American crows play "catch" over the end zone with a crumpled ball of paper. One crow, pursued by all the others, carried the ball in its claws. When the "quarterback" released the ball, another crow caught it with its feet in midair, and the whole game began again. In Japan, jungle crows are known to collect dried deer poop . . . and stuff it into the deer's ears. For no apparent reason.

Are these birds potential tool inventors? Or juvenile delinquents? You be the judge.

In New Caledonia, the local crows found themselves in an unusual situation. There were lots of wood-boring grubs on the island. Anywhere else, woodpeckers would be the dominant grub eaters, but there weren't any woodpeckers in New Caledonia. The grubs were up for grabs. Crows don't have rock-hard

One crow scientist jokingly refers to New Caledonian crows as "bad woodpeckers."

bills made for wood drilling, so this environment could have favored harder-billed crows. Eventually a crow with a wood-pecker-like bill might have evolved. Instead, the crows of New Caledonia used their intelligence to invent wood-probing tools. It was a true triumph of brains over brawn. Gavin suspects that the crows started off using sticks and leaf stems and then added pandanus tools.

⌃ Gavin finds a tool outline left behind on a pandanus leaf.

Gavin looks up into a pandanus plant. The plants are found in many parts of New Caledonia.

35

Have New Caledonian crows improved their tools over time? To find out, Gavin needs to collect as many tools as possible. It's hard work. Even when he sees a bird drop a tool, he may have trouble locating it. "Sometimes I search the forest floor for hours before I find it," Gavin says.

Luckily, pandanus tools can be studied long after both the tool and the toolmaking crow are no longer on the scene. Gavin leads us downhill into a green weave of vines, shrubs, and trees punctuated with spiky pandanus plants. He quickly spots telltale cuts and tears on a leaf.

"After the crow tears off the tool, it leaves behind a matching outline on the pandanus leaf," Gavin explains. "There's a history of tool manufacture on the pandanus plants."

Gavin also wanted to know exactly how the crows make pandanus tools. So, with the help of his students, he built a feeding station and filled holes in a log with small pieces of raw meat. An uprooted pandanus plant was set nearby to provide the crows with raw materials for tools.

Gavin discovered that a pandanus toolmaker starts work by making a short vertical snip against the grain of the stringy veins running through the leaf. Next, the crow rips the leaf horizontally, following the grain. Another snip is required in order to detach the tool. Some crows make stepped tools—with as many as four "steps"—by a sequence of snip-rip-snip-rip-snip-rip-snip-rip-snip. The stepped design allows the bird to make a tapered tool out of a material that can't be torn diagonally because of the leaf's stringy veins. The crow holds the wider end of the stepped pandanus tool in its bill and uses the thinner end to probe crevices that might hide an insect, worm, spider, or small lizard.

After a quick demonstration by Gavin, I'm inspired to make

POSSIBLE EVOLUTION OF THE PANDANUS TOOL

1. A crow rips at a pandanus leaf while foraging for hidden prey.

2. The first pandanus tools were probably wide. A wide tool is stiff and easy to hold, but the tip is too big to reach into small crevices.

my own stepped tool. Equipped with my largish brain and nimble fingers, I create what is surely the perfect pandanus probe.

"Um, no," Gavin says, squinting at my handiwork. "You started from the wrong end. You have to orient the tool so the barbed edge points *upward.*"

I guess practice makes perfect. During a two-year study, Gavin and his student Jennifer Holzhaider watched six juvenile crows gradually learn the craft of pandanus toolmaking. At first the young crows ripped leaves randomly. But like Little Feather, they also followed their parents and watched intently. They tried out their parents' discarded tools; they experimented with snips and rips. By seven months, all the youngsters could make serviceable tools. One seven-month-old bird (showoff!) could make pandanus tools as well as the adults. Late bloomers took as long as two years to master the skill.

Gavin thinks that the invention of the pandanus tool happened this way: A crow, already experienced with stick tools, was ripping at a pandanus leaf in an effort to get at a bug hiding in the crevice between the leaf and the pandanus stem. As it held a torn piece of pandanus in its bill, that crafty crow realized that this strip could also work as a tool.

"It would be nice to show that pandanus tools started with a simple ripped tool of equal width at top and bottom and then gradually improved into a tapered tool by the addition of the steps," says Gavin. "But that's difficult to show."

For the past twenty years Gavin has been visiting two sites about 200 kilometers (120 miles) apart. In both places the crows make pandanus tools, but the step-tool design is different. Every four years Gavin visits each site to collect "counterparts" of pandanus toolmaking left behind on the leaves. He has

3. Next comes the one-step tool. The holding end is wide; the business end is narrow.

4. A tapered, multi-step tool is the best: stiff and easy to hold at the top, more flexible in the middle, and narrow at the tip. (Notice the outline of the tool left behind on the leaf.)

Different communities of crows in New Caledonia make different kinds of pandanus tools. Since the birds are all very similar, and the environments are very similar as well, the differences in the kinds of tools they make are probably social traditions. In other words, crows may have distinct cultures.

already gathered some five thousand counterparts. He wants to know if the shape or size or orientation (leaves torn from the left or from the right) of the tool changes over time. It may take many more years of data collection—perhaps decades of data collection—to detect changes in pandanus toolmaking.

"Do crows move from a two-step design to a three-step design or in the other direction? Or do the tools stay the same?" Gavin wonders.

Humans once stood atop the ONLY SPECIES THAT MAKES TOOLS pedestal. We got knocked off by a chimp. Now we stand atop the ONLY SPECIES THAT IMPROVES TOOL TECHNOLOGY AND PASSES ON THOSE IMPROVEMENTS pedestal. Enjoy this distinction while it lasts! Someday we might get nudged off by a crow.

TOOL USE BY THE NUMBERS

Approximate number of known animal species:	1,371,500
Number of animal species observed using tools:	284
Number of animal species observed making or modifying tools:	42
Number of animal species known to make multiple kinds of tools (*humans, chimpanzees, orangutans, capuchin monkeys, and New Caledonian crows*):	5
Number of animal species known to make hooked tools (*humans and New Caledonian crows*):	2

« Gavin prepares a tempting feast for the crows. The black line is a roll of netting that is designed to spring up and over the birds.

CAPTURE DAY.

Gavin set up the net in the wee hours of the morning. An innocent ring of black cord now circles the log, which we've baited with grubs, raw beef, and cracked-open chicken eggs. This "whoosh net" is Gavin's creation. Catching forest birds can be quite difficult because of the lack of open space. Gavin designed his net so that when he pulls a cord, the edges will go up and in, like a giant drawstring bag.

Sometimes Gavin enlists his family in his crow-catching efforts. His wife, Megan, and ten-year-old daughter, Frances, have helped band crows in New Caledonia. Back home in New Zea-

39

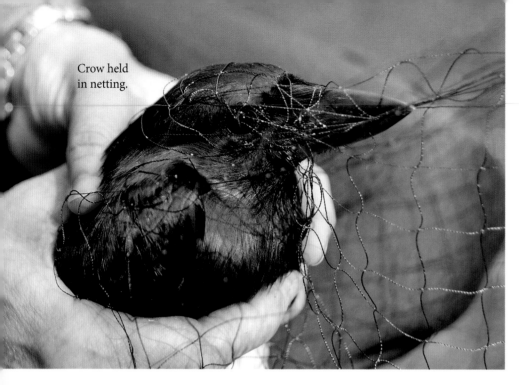
Crow held in netting.

land, Gavin tested this new net on his seven-year-old son, Robert, and on George, the family cat. "Robert enjoyed being netted," says Gavin. "George wasn't so happy."

Studying crows often requires capturing them in whoosh nets. Gavin and his students were able to find out how long it takes young crows to learn pandanus toolmaking by capturing and color banding each crow in the study area. Without these bands, it would have been impossible to tell the crows apart.

We wait quietly in the blind. Little Feather's family seems to make several swings a day through this part of the forest. It's only a matter of time . . .

Whoo-whoo-whoo. Wings whistle as a lone crow settles on the log. Gavin jerks the net's release cord, but not quite hard enough. Before he can give a second tug, the crow rockets into the treetops with a startled *WAAK! WAAK!*

Does this shout *It's a trap!* to any crows within earshot? Hopefully crow communication isn't quite that sophisticated. We reset everything and wait.

Thirty minutes later, two crows glide in for a landing. They eye the big yellow yolks of the chicken eggs . . .

Whoosh!

Gavin's timing is perfect. One crow is caught near the ground and the other is snagged as it tries to launch upward. I was expecting loud corvid curses, but neither bird gives a single squawk of protest as we disentangle them. They don't struggle much, either.

Each bird goes into a cloth bag while Gavin prepares his equipment. When everything is ready, I ease the first bird out. From its size, Gavin guesses it's an adult male. Little Feather's father, perhaps?

Gavin fixes a numbered metal band to the crow's leg, and two different-colored bands for easy ID. I gently spread one of the crow's wings. Its feathers are gorgeous—ebony with a silky sheen, like glamorous evening wear.

Using a tiny needle, Gavin extracts a blood sample from a vein on the inside of the crow's wing. A genetic analysis of the bird's blood will confirm its sex and tell the scientists how closely this crow is related to crows living elsewhere in New Caledonia.

I return Crow Number One to its bag and bring out Crow Number Two. It blinks in the sudden sunlight and soundlessly opens its bill. The inside of the crow's mouth is slightly reddish. Baby crows have red mouths, a handy bull's-eye for Mom or Dad when stuffing bugs down their kids' throats. As the young crow

≪ The crow is banded with both numbered metal bands and colored bands.

41

<< Gavin takes a blood sample. Although male New Caledonian crows are slightly bigger and heavier than females, it's impossible to be sure of a crow's sex without seeing mating behavior or taking blood for a genetic test.

vidual crows apart, crows are astonishingly good at recognizing individual human faces.

University of Washington researchers captured, banded, and released several American crows that lived on their campus. Since captured crows had previously scolded and dive-bombed people who captured them, the researchers wore plastic caveman masks to hide their identities. Later they tested the crows by walking around campus wearing caveman masks. The crows continued to dive-bomb and scold the people wearing the masks, even if the people also wore hats or put the masks on

⋁ The juvenile crow is measured. Gavin and his colleagues want to know if there are any significant physical differences among crows living in different parts of New Caledonia. So far, it appears that the differences are more cultural than physical.

grows up, the inside of its mouth fades to gray. Could this youngster be Little Feather? Maybe. The crow doesn't have a small twisted feather on its left shoulder, but the plume might have fallen out or been straightened by preening. Family members sometimes run their bills through each other's feathers. It's one of the ways they express their tight social bonds.

Gavin measures the youngster's head and bill. The young crow endures everything without protest. But the adult has had enough of us. When it's time to be measured, the crow squirms, tries to bite the measuring calipers, and gives me the evil eye.

I have a feeling this bird's going to remember me . . . and not fondly. Although humans have a hard time telling indi-

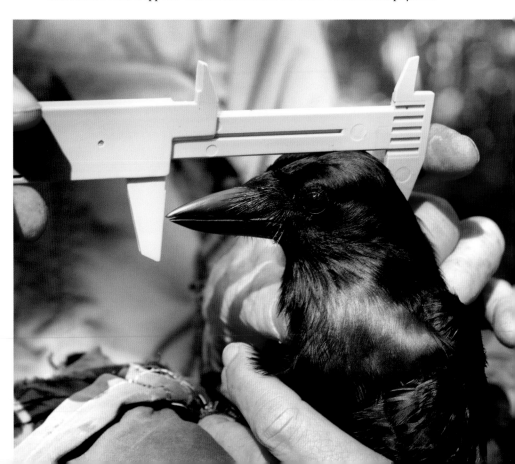

their heads upside down. The crows didn't react to the researchers when they wore a different kind of mask or didn't wear any mask at all. Over time, as the offspring of the original crows grew up, they learned a lesson from their parents: Watch out for dangerous cavemen! Eight years later, the campus crows still got angry at anyone wearing the mask.

Gavin has finished his measuring, so I hand the crow over. Gavin holds up the bird and slowly opens his hands. The crow flies into a nearby tree, clearly glad to be free, but not panicked. Next, Gavin releases the younger bird. Both crows immediately begin pecking at the colored bands now latched to their legs. The juvenile dances along the branch as if trying to hop out of its unwelcome jewelry.

By way of apology, we leave the rest of our chopped meat, grubs, and cracked-open chicken eggs on the log. It's a regular Crow Café (Caw-fé?).

Next we're heading to the aviaries, where birds netted several months before are being tested in order to understand more about crow smarts. We know that wild crows use tools. But can a crow use a tool to solve problems it has never faced in the wild?

We pack up and hike along the forest path back to Gavin's truck. I have a bad feeling about this. I expect dive-bombings and angry alarm calls, maybe even rotten candlenuts or gooey eggshells dropped on our heads.

Yet we escape unscathed. I'm very happy to be in New Caledonia, where the crows, it seems, don't hold grudges.

The crow heads for the trees.

Field studies of wild crows are examples of observational science. Lab studies of captive crows are examples of experimental science. Both help researchers understand how New Caledonian crows think. Field studies show why the crows use tools. Lab studies reveal abilities that aren't obvious in the crows' natural environment.

5 METATOOLS AND MIND TRICKS

THE LAST THING YOU EXPECT TO HEAR FROM A CROW IS A CATLIKE *MAUW*. Yet as we draw near the aviaries, all I hear is soft *mauw . . . mauw*ing. As if the cages were filled with bored kittens.

"That's the sound they make in close quarters," Gavin explains. "A low-key keeping-in-touch call."

The dozen crows mewing to each another are from two different parts of New Caledonia. I wonder—does each group think that the others talk with a funny accent?

We enter a T-shaped central hallway that has cages on either side. The enclosures are tall: in order to feel safe, crows need to perch above people's heads.

"Unless a bird is sick and needs veterinary treatment, we don't handle them while they're here," Gavin says. He shows us a wooden frame set atop a small scale. "We put meat on the scale and put it in the cage, so when a bird lands on top of the scale, we can get its weight without touching it. That way we know that they're healthy and eating well."

The dozen birds living here are helping Gavin and Russell Gray and Alex Taylor, his colleagues at the University of Auckland, learn more about crow intelligence. New Caledonian crows certainly have an impressive physical tool kit of sticks, leaf stems, and pandanus strips. Do they have an equally impressive mental tool kit? Can they reason, remember, and figure things out?

The three crows housed behind Aviary Number One are enrolled in an experiment that attempts to teach them to make uniquely shaped objects. The birds came from an area with lots of pandanus plants. If these crows can craft pandanus tools, can they learn to make objects with other shapes? If they can, this would show just how flexible their intelligence is, and how much they rely on reason and learning.

Two of the crows are skipping restlessly from perch to perch.

The third, fiddling with the end of the plastic cable that secures the perch to the cage, twists the skinny plastic around like a Boy Scout attempting a difficult knot. Like monkeys and Border collies, crows seem happiest when they are busy.

Behind Aviary Number Two, across the hallway, a solo crow plays with one of the strings that hang from its perches. A bit of raw meat is tied to the end of the string. This bird failed at even the simplest experimental tasks, so it's given "enrichment activities" like this to keep it from getting bored. The not-so-smart crow will remain in the aviary, enjoying meals of soaked cat kibble, chopped meat, raw eggs, fruit, and other goodies until it can be released alongside the other crows it was captured with.

All food and no real work. Hmmm. Maybe this bird *isn't* a dunce. Maybe it's a candidate for the Smart Crow Hall of Fame. (This doesn't exist, sadly, but we can dream.) But if there were a Smart Crow Hall of Fame, the first inductee would surely be a bird named Betty. About fourteen years ago she rocked the scientific world.

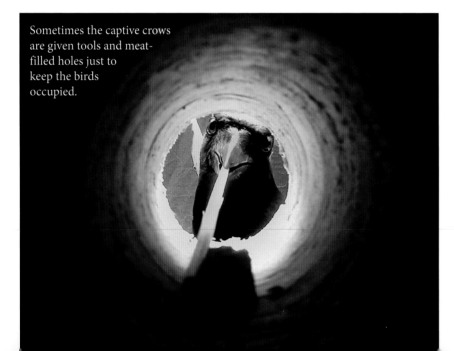

Sometimes the captive crows are given tools and meat-filled holes just to keep the birds occupied.

⋀ Betty the crow.

GAVIN'S DISCOVERIES OF WILD TOOL-USING CROWS INSPIRED ALEX KACELNIK, a scientist at the University of Oxford, to study the crows in captivity. He received permission to take several crows back to England. Betty was caught near Yaté (YAH-tay), a small town of about a thousand people that is located in the southeast of New Caledonia. Betty's cagemate, Abel, was a male who had lived in the New Caledonian Zoo for about ten years. Alex Kacelnik hoped to test the birds' intelligence through carefully controlled experiments that would be impossible in the wild. How much of the crows' toolmaking and tool-using ability was instinctive? How much was based on reasoning? If New Caledonian crows were truly intelligent, they should be able to recognize a usable tool even if it was made from an unfamiliar material.

Betty and Abel were given a puzzle. A clear tube was taped to a plastic bin. At the bottom of the tube rested a tiny bucket. A chunk of raw pig heart—one of the crows' favorite treats—had been set inside the bucket. The Oxford researchers also put two pieces of wire in the enclosure. The end of one wire was bent into a hook; the other was straight. A wild crow's natural tools are always made of plant material, not cold, slippery metal. Would the crows realize that the hooked wire was a usable tool? Would they understand that the straight wire was useless?

Abel flew to the table. He snatched the hooked wire. But instead of sticking it down the tube, he flew off to the other side of the aviary to play with it.

⚓ Betty's bent-wire act was no fluke. In nine out of ten trials she successfully bent the wire and pulled out the bucket. Later, when given curved strips of aluminum that didn't fit down the tube, Betty created a useful tool by straightening and rebending the strips.

Betty picked up the straight wire. She carried it to the tube and fished around. No go. So she pulled it back out. She stuck the end of the wire into the sticky tape that held the tube down. Betty tugged a bit and then pulled out the wire, which was now bent into a hook at one end. She stuck it down the tube and pulled up the bucket.

The scientists ran more trials. Nine out of ten times, Betty either used the sticky tape to hold the wire as she bent it, or she held the wire in her feet as she bent it with her bill.

Was the first trial just a fluke? Maybe that first time Betty just happened to get the wire stuck and ended up with a hook. Maybe she was a quick learner who recognized a happy accident and took advantage.

The other possibility is that Betty used insight to solve the problem. She didn't just see what the wire *was*; she saw what it *could be.*

Human children given a similar test didn't do as well as Betty did. In the human experiment, children were given a straight pipe cleaner that could be bent into a hook to retrieve a bucket. Out of 24 children age four and five, only 2 (8 percent) were at Betty's level. When 27 children age six and seven were tested, only 8 (30 percent) could solve the problem.

However, the problem wasn't *exactly* the same as Betty's, because the children's bucket held a colorful sticker. Sorry, kids—no pig hearts for you!

As Betty's genius was being revealed, Gavin and Russell Gray and Alex Taylor at the University of Auckland were beginning their own experiments with captive New Caledonian crows. For humans, part of using tools is understanding that objects have certain properties (thickness, heaviness, density, etc.). Once we understand an object's properties, we can be smart about how we use it.

Alex and Russell gave captive crows a puzzle they called the Aesop's Fable test. In the fable, a thirsty crow comes across a pitcher with a bit of water at the bottom. Unable to reach the water, the crow thinks of an ingenious solution: he drops stones into the pitcher until the water level is high enough for him to drink. The moral is "Think, think, and you'll get a drink."

New Caledonian crows don't use stones as tools in the wild, so the crows first had to be taught stone dropping. Once they mastered dropping stones into a tube to collapse a platform that delivered a treat, the crows were given their first Aesop's test. The five New Caledonian crows were presented with two clear tubes and a scattered collection of small stones. One tube held water; inside the tube, a bit of meat was attached to a small float. The other tube was the same, except the treat rested on sand. Both sand and water were at the same level, a few inches lower than the height the birds could reach with their bill.

The crows quickly learned to drop the stones into the water-filled tube. The birds performed better than five-year-old children given a similar task.

Next, the sand-filled tube and the stones were taken away.

This time the crows had the choice between two types of rectangles they could drop into the water-filled tube. The rectangles were the same size, color, and shape, but were made of two different materials. One was rubber and heavy enough to sink (and raise the water level). The other was lightweight plastic that floated. The crows had no problem figuring out which kind of rectangle to drop into the tube. One bird *never* dropped a lightweight rectangle into the tube. It picked up the light rectangle sixteen times but always discarded it. Overall, the New Caledonian crows outperformed seven-year-old children who were given the same test.

In the third part of the test, the rectangles were taken away. This time the crows were given squares of equal size, weight, and color. However, one type of square was an open metal frame

⋏ The U-tube experiment tests the crow's ability to understand hidden connections.

(which sank, without much effect on the water level) while the other was made of hardened clay. Again the crows quickly learned to drop only the solid squares. Two of the five crows *never* dropped a hollow square into the tube. (Children weren't given this test, so we don't know how the birds' performance would have compared.)

The final test was truly tough. This time there were three tubes. The treat was in a narrow middle tube, which was flanked by two wider tubes. Stones could be dropped into the wider tubes but wouldn't fit into the tube holding the treat. *One* of the side tubes was connected to the middle tube via a hidden "U-tube" under the platform. The only way of figuring out the connection was to carefully watch the water level of the middle tube; it went up slightly when a stone was placed in the correct side tube.

Alas! None of the crows could figure it out. When this same test was given to children, four- and five-year-olds were as stumped as the crows were. Six-year-olds breezed through. Score one for human children!

⋏ A crow chooses a solid square, rather than a hollow square of the same weight, in order to bring a floating treat within reach.

NATURE VERSUS NURTURE

Let's say you're a shy person. Are you shy because you were born that way? Or did you grow up having experiences that molded your personality in that direction? This is what scientists call the nature versus nurture debate.

With New Caledonian crows, scientists wondered: How much of their tool behavior is "hardwired" in their genes? How much is because of their upbringing? To sort that out, the University of Oxford researchers hand-raised four New Caledonian crows. One of the baby crows was Betty's daughter, Uék (pronounced "Wek"; it means "bird" in the Kanak language of New Caledonia). Uék and her cagemate were given sticks to play with. A log with treat-filled holes was placed in their aviary. Every day a human came in and used the sticks to pull treats out of the holes for the youngsters. Uék and her cagemate watched and learned. Two other human-raised crows had the same aviary setup and the same amount of human attention, with one exception: none of the humans ever handled a tool-like object. These two birds were "untutored."

Uék and her cagemate learned how to get food with a stick tool. This

≪ Betty's daughter Uék is tutored by a human caretaker.

⌃ Baby New Caledonian crows.

wasn't surprising, as they had watched humans do it. But the untutored birds also figured out how to use the sticks to pull food out of the holes, despite never having seen a human (or another crow) use any kind of tool. When given pandanus leaves, one of the untutored birds even managed to tear off a strip of pandanus and use it as a tool. This suggests that all New Caledonian crows are born with some sort of tool-using ability.

On the other hand, none of the four human-raised birds ever managed to make more sophisticated tools, such as hooked sticks or stepped pandanus tools. This implies that young crows need to learn complex toolmaking by watching their parents.

It seems that among New Caledonian crows, sophisticated toolmaking requires both nature *and* nurture.

BACK AT THE AVIARIES, GAVIN INTRODUC-
ES ANDY COMINS AND ME to graduate student
Guido De Filippo. Guido leads us along the aviary hallway. Sunlight drizzles through the netting
of the enclosure holding three of Guido's study birds. Munin,
Hugin, and Spoon are banded yellow, white, and red, respective-
ly, for easy identification.

These study birds and three other crows were caught about
four months earlier near Yaté, where the famous Betty was captured. They might even be her relatives. Of the three birds in the
enclosure, Spoon is the shiest. She got her name because the
tip of her upper bill is broken off. She can't hold things as well
as other crows and has to scoop up food with her lower bill. Yet
somehow, despite her disability, Spoon has managed to survive
in the wild.

A "bird door" is built into the top edge of the crows' aviary.
Guido uses a long pole to slide it open. Hugin, the white-band-
ed bird, pops out almost instantly. She glides down the hallway
over our heads toward the experimental room where the crows
are tested. The experimental room also has a bird door at the
top as well as a larger people door. Gavin designed intercon-
nected aviaries, hallways, and experimental rooms so that the
birds can be gently shooed from one area to another without
being handled.

Hugin ignores the bird door and zips through the people
door. "Yeah, she likes the big door better," says Guido. "They're
quirky birds."

Guido opens a bird door.

51

Munin also ignores the bird door to the experimental room. Instead he lands on a small table in the hallway. Right next to a plastic container full of chopped meat.

"He likes to eat," says Guido. "He'll do fifty experimental trials in a row just for the snacks!"

He shoos Hugin back into her enclosure as Munin flies through the bird door into the experimental room. Guido named Hugin and Munin after two legendary ravens. In Norse mythology, Hugin and Munin ("Thought" and "Memory") flew around the world as the spies of the great god Odin, winging home to whisper news into his ears. Obviously, this happened in the dark days before the gods had Internet service.

"Hugin perches close behind me when I'm setting up things in the experimental room, so I feel almost like Odin with a bird on my shoulder," says Guido.

Guido grew up in Italy, where his dad is a veterinarian and his mom works with disabled children. "I was around animals early on, and also around people who couldn't always express what they were thinking," Guido says. When he was a child, he read a book called *King Solomon's Ring* by Konrad Lorenz, a famous animal behavior scientist. "Lorenz wrote about the King Solomon fable. King Solomon had a ring that allowed him to talk to animals," says Guido. "But talking to animals like you would talk to a person is too easy. It's more interesting to figure out other ways of knowing what an animal is thinking."

Guido has offered to show us something called the metatool experiment. As he sets up the apparatus, I peek through a spy hole into the adjoining aviary. This smaller enclosure holds

Seashell Collector, another of Guido's study birds. Seashell Collector pauses to stare at me. All the aviaries are dirt-floored, with sand and coral rubble mixed in. Guido told me that Seashell Collector likes to pluck tiny shells out of the dirt and store them in her food and water dishes. If she were human, we would say that Seashell Collector has a hobby.

All birds have piercing gazes, but a crow's stare can pin you to a wall. Seashell Collector looks at me as though she's attempting a Jedi mind trick.

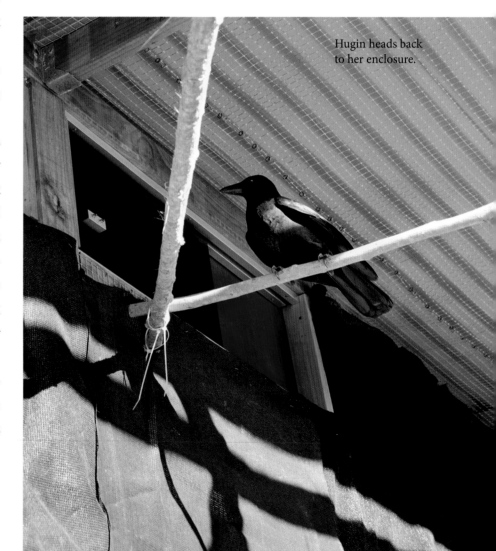

Hugin heads back to her enclosure.

⌃ Guido with Hugin (foreground), Munin, and Spoon. "'I like the idea that we are changing how people think about crows," says Guido. "People associate them with dark things—horror films, and how crows used to follow armies and eat the dead bodies. But crows are amazing! Silky and sleek and smart."

Guido is both a scientist and an artist. He sprinkles his notes with sketches of crows. He also created all of the artwork in this book!

53

a crow figure out how to use a tool to get a tool to get food?

Guido has placed a Plexiglas rectangle and a slatted box on the table in the experimental room. Inside the Plexiglas is a bit of meat. A long stick lies on the table. Munin flies over and examines the rectangle closely. He picks up the stick, flies to the perch, and promptly drops the stick.

The door opens and Guido enters. When the birds are in the experimental room, they are given only a few moments to do

I glance down. A petite, perfect snow-white cowrie shell lies in the dirt at my feet. I pick it up and push it through the cage wire. Seashell Collector is a bit startled, as if she can't believe what just happened. Her head bobs as she glances from the cowrie to me and back to the cowrie. I know she won't feel safe coming to the ground while I'm pressed against the netting, so I move away. Immediately I hear the *whisk* of wings. Seashell Collector nabs my offering and flies up to her water dish. *Plonk*.

Next door, Guido is ready to give Munin a shot at the metatool puzzle. A metatool is a tool used to make another tool, or a tool used to get another tool. It's one thing to use a tool to get food; we know wild New Caledonian crows can do that. But can

To prepare Munin for the metatool test, Guido will first let the crow get comfortable with the test set-up.

54

Guido puts meat on the string . . . which Munin promptly pulls up, using a bill-and-foot technique.

whatever it is they are going to do. The birds need to know that they can either perform or not perform, but they don't have much time. Otherwise the experimental room becomes a play-room. Fun for the crows, but not so great if you're a graduate student who needs to run dozens—sometimes hundreds—of trials to gather data.

Guido places the stick back on the table. As soon as Guido leaves, Munin picks up the stick and delicately maneuvers out the meat chunk. No problem.

This time Guido enters and ties a long string to the one of the perches and knots a small piece of meat to the other end. Crows in the wild don't pull up dangling strings. Yet Munin doesn't hesitate. He reaches down and grabs the string with his bill, pulls it up, and holds the string with his foot while he hauls up the rest of the string. After chucking down the tidbit, Munin continues pecking at the knot and manages to rip off a bit of string. Guido has to follow Munin around the cage until the crow drops it.

The next step is to tie both a short stick and a piece of meat to the end of the string. Munin retrieves the meat, pulls off the short stick, and flies to the table to eye the new treat Guido has placed inside the Plexiglas. The crow seems to realize that the short stick is too short, because he doesn't even try to use it. Instead Munin drops it and flies to the ground. He seems to be searching for a longer tool.

I ask Guido what fascinates him the most about crows. "It's the link between the evolution of toolmaking and the evolution of language," he explains. "In humans, the areas of the brain that are active during toolmaking are almost identical to the areas of the brain that are active during speech."

Scientists recently used brain scans to discover this link. It might seem odd, but both making tools and forming words require fine motor control. In toolmaking it's fine motor control of hands and fingers; during speech it's fine motor control of lips and tongue. (Notice the tiny differences between saying "cat" and "bat.")

It may have happened this way: over three million years ago our early human ancestors began making tools. It was an important survival skill. In every generation those who were better at toolmaking tended to leave behind more descendants. Our environment favored individuals with bigger brains, brains with better fine motor control. Once our tool lifestyle had produced the necessary brain wiring, so to speak, we could do other things with the same circuitry. Complex language became possible.

Tools may have made humans smart *and* chatty. What about crows? Very little is known about the sounds they make and what those sounds might mean.

"All this intelligence—where is evolution driving the crow brain?" asks Guido. "Their brains and bodies are going in the direction of being better and better at toolmaking and tool using. Will it drive crows to do other things? Will they develop complex language?"

In the experimental room, Munin is now being given the complete metatool puzzle. Guido has tied a short stick to the end of a string. The table holds the Plexiglas with a treat pushed deep inside. The slotted box is no longer empty. Now it holds a long stick, though the stick is out of reach of Munin's bill.

Munin hauls up the string and pulls off the short stick. He

⌃ Munin grabs the short stick and flies down to the slotted box that holds the long stick.

glides over with the short stick in his mouth. We hear the *tap-tap-tap* of little feet on the experimental table as Munin moves back and forth between the Plexiglas and the slotted box.

"You can almost hear the gears turning in his brain," Guido whispers.

Munin pauses. Maybe Guido's setup is too hard. When Munin faces the slotted box, he has to turn away from the Plexiglas box with its juicy treat. Maybe he won't be able to remember his ultimate goal. Honestly, I can sympathize. Sometimes I set down my cell phone and three seconds later I can't remember where I put it.

But no—Munin picks up the short stick. He sticks it through the slats and delicately maneuvers one end of the long stick close. He drops the short stick and pulls out the long one. Munin whips

around. The last part is easy! For his final flourish, he perches atop the Plexiglas. Using an acrobatic upside-down technique, he maneuvers the beef chunk out and gulps it down.

This three-part puzzle wasn't a problem. What if we gave Munin a four-part problem or a five-part problem? I wish this crow's brain were wired for human speech. I imagine him saying, *Bring it on! As long as you bring the beef.*

⌃ Munin uses the short stick to get the long stick to get the treat.

An idyllic beach on
New Caledonia.

6 HOMECOMING

Tolie, Issaï, and Adolphe.

OUR TWO-CAR CARAVAN FOLLOWS A WINDING ROAD. Gavin is in the lead, driving the project's truck with its crow cargo: Munin, Hugin, Spoon, Seashell Collector, and Crow We Never Got Around to Naming.

Andy and I follow Gavin's truck. Here in the southeast of New Caledonia the landscape is stark, with stunted plants and rusty-red dirt. The southeast is home to some of the nickel mines that provide much of New Caledonia's wealth.

After several hours' drive, we run out of highway. Just past Yaté, we run out of paved road. Gavin parks on a wide lawn in front of a tidy house that has a large outdoor kitchen. Adolphe Ouetcho comes out to greet us, accompanied by his wife, Tolie, and their youngest grandchild, a two-year-old dynamo named Issaï. Both of Issaï's parents work at the local nickel mine. Five months earlier, Adolphe helped Gavin capture all five of the birds sitting in Gavin's truck. Now Adolphe is going to help deliver them home.

We drive farther. We run out of dirt road, and then we run out of dirt. Knee-deep water separates us from the islet where the crows were captured. Adolphe has brought along a small inflatable raft to float the birds across. We set the five plastic crow carriers (that look suspiciously like cat carriers) in the raft and shade them with a plastic tarp.

Adolphe has been visiting the crows' islet all his life. He explains that crows in New Caledonia don't get much respect. "Crows are considered a bad omen. And they announce people's coming, sort of like an alarm bird." Which is not appreciated when the local people visit the crows' islet to hunt forest pigeons and fruit bats.

Adolphe points out the islet where the crows were captured.

Many New Caledonians are surprised to find out that wild crows use tools. Adolphe says he has seen crows drop snails on rocks to break the shells, and he remembers that when he was younger, old people told stories about crows using tools. "We didn't believe them," he says. Five months ago he helped Gavin set up a feeding station to capture these crows. There, for the first time, he saw crows using tools. "Now we are learning together," Adolphe says.

The shallow water gets shallower and turns into mud flats, so we hand-carry the crow carriers. I'm squelching across with Seashell Collector. Every once in a while she gives a short *waak-waak* call. Maybe she's getting an occasional splash of salt water (sorry), feeling the indignity of being in a cat carrier (it's not my fault!), and calling me a scruffy-looking nerf-herder (clearly I am reading way too much into a few *waak-waak*s).

We reach the islet and tromp through the thick underbrush to a clearing fringed by coconut trees. We all agree that it will be a nice spot for the release because the birds will have space to fly. In the distance we hear the ocean bashing itself rhythmically against the fringing reef.

Gavin takes Hugin out of her carrier. She blinks in the sudden sunlight and twists her head around to stare. He waits a few moments to let her get her bearings before slowly opening his hands.

Hugin makes a big swoop upward and lands in a coconut tree not twenty feet away. *Waak*, she says tentatively, followed by a few more contact calls: *Waak. Waak.*

Adolphe gets ready to release Munin.

61

Next Gavin sends Crow We Never Got Around to Naming into the sky. He also settles among the coconut fronds.

Adolphe cradles Spoon in his hands. As soon as he opens them, she flies up to join Hugin and Crow We Never Got Around to Naming. The three of them are *waak*ing it up, getting louder and more excited, as if they just realized where they are. From somewhere in the distance comes an answer: *Waak*. The three crows fly toward the sound, calling *Waak, waak, waak*.

Now it's Munin's turn. Our star puzzle solver squirms and squawks, and Adolphe lets him fly. Munin rests for only a moment in the coconut tree before bolting in the same direction as the other birds.

Gavin takes Seashell Collector out of her carrier. Seashell Collector is already looking inland, toward the *waak-waak* sounds. When Gavin releases her, she arcs into the sky and disappears.

Gavin examines Spoon's bill. Her upper bill is broken at the tip. Despite her disability, she's a survivor.

Seashell Collector takes flight.

I glance down. Seashell Collector's home, I suddenly realize, is littered with crunchy white coral and tiny cowrie shells.

We can no longer see Hugin, Crow We Never Got Around to Naming, Spoon, Munin, and Seashell Collector. But judging from the volume of *waak waak waak*s coming from the treetops, every crow on the islet has gathered to greet them.

"It's a welcome home party," says Adolphe. "The family is back together again."

Home at last.

63

Hugin perches in her aviary. The scientists work with captive, wild-caught crows only during the New Caledonian winter, so as not to disrupt the birds' breeding season.

ASK THE AUTHOR

Q: You seem to love crows. Why?

A: I volunteer at Lindsay Wildlife Hospital in Walnut Creek, California, and one busy day I was given the task of syringe-feeding an enclosure full of juvenile crows. As I fed my first baby crow, it let out a high-pitched glug-glug-glug. It was such a ridiculous sound that I fell instantly in love.

Over the past few years I've hand-raised many baby crows. They are obsessively interested in *everything*. No newspaper goes unripped. No food goes unplayed with. If one crow has something, the other crow wants it. They are awesomely naughty.

Q: Do you really think crows recognize individual people?

A: I can personally vouch for their ability. I've visited my hand-raised crows months after they've moved on to a big aviary and are living with other crows. My hand-raised crows will perch near me and give begging calls, mouths open and wings fluffing. But they won't go near anybody else. And although my former wards clearly recognize me, I'm embarrassed to say I don't recognize them. I have to look at their leg bands.

Pamela Turner with Tolie,
Véronique, Issaï, Adolphe,
and Gavin.

This crow likes to hold its tool along the right side of its head. New Caledonian crows and humans are the only species that show strong "handedness" or "laterality" when using tools.

Q: WHAT'S THE BEST THING ABOUT RAISING BABY CROWS?

A: The best part is letting them go. I box them up (which they don't like) and take them to our veterinary staff for one last checkup (which they also don't like). I drive out to a nice spot in a rural area with big gum trees, a year-round stream, and lots of other crows, and then I gently let them go. That part they like.

Q: WHAT SHOULD I DO IF I FIND A BABY CROW OR SOME OTHER BABY BIRD?

A: Sometimes people mistakenly "rescue" fledgling birds. But many young birds go through a stage when they're out of the nest and perching, but not yet able to fly. These birds are usually being taken care of by their parents. If you find a fledgling on the ground, it's best to put the youngster up in a tree or a bush, keep your dogs and cats inside, and watch to see if the parents arrive. If a bird of any age has been caught by a cat, however, it's best to bring the bird to a place that cares for injured wildlife. Tiny teeth punctures can easily become infected. And if you have a cat, it's best to make it an indoor cat. It will live much longer and so will all the neighborhood birds.

I highly recommend the Cornell Lab of Ornithology's information on rescuing (or not rescuing) baby crows and other baby birds at **www.birds.cornell.edu/crows/babycrow.htm**.

Q: I REALLY WONDER IF YOU MADE UP ALL THIS CRAZY CROW STUFF. HOW DO YOU *KNOW*? CAN YOU PROVIDE EVIDENCE?

A: Ah, a skeptic! You should consider science as a career. "How do you know?" is at the heart of all scientific debates. It is, in fact, a great general-purpose question. Sure, asking "How do you know?" will get you into trouble. Even when voiced very, very politely, eventually somebody will take offense at having to give evidence for something they are spouting off. Do it anyway. Asking that question is a great way of separating truth from half-truth and untruth.

When a scientist makes a claim, he or she anticipates that other scientists are going to ask "How do you know?"

When scientists discover new information, either by observing something in nature or doing an experiment, or both, they write a scientific paper. These papers are reviewed by other scientists who are looking to see if the author has been rigorous in collecting data and has interpreted the data correctly. If the paper passes muster, it's published in a scientific journal. A paper tells (often in mind-numbing detail) what the scientists did and what results were found, and discuss what the results might mean. In short, a scientific paper provides the evidence demanded of a scientist by other scientists.

In the Selected Bibliography I've listed the scientific papers that were most important in writing this book; you can find a more extensive list on my website (**www.pamelasturner.com**). Just go to the *Crow Smarts* page. I also recommend exploring the University of Auckland's Cognition and Culture in New Caledonian Crows website at **www.psych.auckland.ac.nz/en/about/our-research/research-groups/new-caledonian-crow-cognition-and-culture-research.html** and Oxford University's Behavioural Ecology Research Group website at **users.ox.ac.uk/~kgroup**. You'll find research papers, photos, videos, and more.

Little Feather is always hungry.

Q: You mention that new experiments with New Caledonian crows were going on in the aviaries when you visited. Can you tell us how they turned out?

A: As soon as the results of those experiments have been published by the scientists, I'll post the news on the *Crow Smarts* page of my website at **www.pamelasturner.com**. I promise you'll find it fascinating.

Q: What if I just want to watch videos of crows doing goofy things?

A: I thought of that too. I have links to funny, silly, and weird crow videos as well as scientific crow videos on my website's *Crow Smarts* page. You can even watch videos of Lefty and Little Feather!

Q: This whole tool-use thing is really fascinating. Are there other books about tool-using animals that you would recommend?

A: I shamelessly recommend my own book about tool-using dolphins: *The Dolphins of Shark Bay* (Houghton Mifflin Harcourt, 2013), for ages ten and up.

Q: How about more books about crows?

A: For kids, I suggest *Crows! Strange and Wonderful* by Laurence Pringle and Bob Marstall (Boyds Mills Press, 2010). For kids who are up for it, John Marzluff has written two books that are at an adult level: *Gifts of the Crow: How Perception, Emotion, and Thought Allow Smart Birds to Behave Like Humans* (Atria, 2012) and *In the Company of Crows and Ravens* (Yale University Press, 2005). Dr. Marzluff is one of the scientists mentioned on page 48 who tested crows' ability to recognize faces by using plastic masks.

My hands-down favorite writing about crows is a short piece by David Quammen, "Has Success Spoiled the Crow? The Puzzling Case File on the World's Smartest Bird." You can find it in *Natural Acts: A Sidelong View of Science and Nature* (W. W. Norton, 2008). This essay is so clever, I suspect that "David Quammen" is really a crow with a laptop.

Q: Why are references to *Star Wars* scattered throughout *Crow Smarts*?

A: I thought of calling a grub Jabba the Hutt, and it snowballed from there. If you're patting yourself on the back because you think you've spotted all the *Star Wars* references, all I can say is: Great, kid. Don't get cocky.

Q: YOU'RE ABOUT TO RUN OUT OF SPACE! AREN'T THERE PEOPLE YOU WOULD LIKE TO THANK?

A: Yes! First and foremost, the photographer Andy Comins and I would like to thank Gavin Hunt for making this book possible. From our first contact through the review of draft manuscripts and photos, Gavin was unfailingly kind, patient, and helpful. It was a great pleasure to get to know him and to tell his story. Guido De Filippo guided us through the aviary side of crow research; it was an extra bonus to discover this impressive young man's gifts as an artist as well as a scientist. The rest of the University of Auckland team—Russell Gray, Alex Taylor, Sarah Jelbert, and Véronique Monjo—generously provided behind-the-scenes support. We are grateful to Adolphe and Tolie Ouetcho for opening their home to us and sharing their thoughts. Alex Kacelnik of the University of Oxford kindly allowed us to use some of his research photos, going far out of his way to find us the images we needed. Many thanks to those who provided additional photos: Gavin Hunt, Brian McClatchy, Sarah Jelbert, Alex Kacelnik, Jennifer Holzhaider, Don Sprecht, and Steve Bloom. I would like to thank my good friends Deborah Underwood, Keely Parrack, Carol Peterson, Nancy Humphrey Case, and Lesley Mandros Bell, who reviewed the draft manuscript to make sure the non–crow-obsessed could understand it. A special note of appreciation to our editor, Erica Zappy, for guiding this book through from start to finish. The design team, Whitney Leader-Picone and the talented folks at YAY!, dedicated many hours to creating a book that makes us proud. For holding down the fort during our three weeks in New Caledonia, I am grateful to my very understanding spouse, Rob Townsend.

Lastly, thanks to all the crows. You are the best and the brightest.

Gavin comes ashore on the crows' islet.

Although some New Caledonian crows use multiple kinds of tools, all crows seem to have a favorite type of tool that they use most of the time.

SELECTED BIBLIOGRAPHY

Bentley-Condit, Vicki K., and E. O. Smith. "Animal Tool Use: Current Definitions and an Updated Comprehensive Catalog." *Behavior* 147, no. 2 (2010): 185–221.

Emery, Nathan J., and Nicola S. Clayton. "The Mentality of Crows: Convergent Evolution of Intelligence in Corvids and Apes." *Science* 306 (December 10, 2004): 1903–7.

Holzhaider, Jennifer C., Gavin R. Hunt, and Russell D. Gray. "The Development of Pandanus Tool Manufacture in Wild New Caledonian Crows." *Behavior* 147 (2010): 553–86.

Holzhaider, J. C., M. D. Sibley, A. H. Taylor, P. J. Singh, R. D. Gray, and G. R. Hunt. "The Social Structure of New Caledonian Crows." *Animal Behaviour* 81 (2011): 83–92.

Hunt, Gavin R. "Manufacture and Use of Hook-Tools by New Caledonian Crows." *Nature* 379 (January 18, 1996): 249–51.

Hunt, Gavin R., Michael C. Corballis, and Russell D. Gray. "Laterality in Tool Manufacture by Crows." *Nature* 414 (December 13, 2001): 707.

Hunt, Gavin R., and Russell D. Gray. "Diversification and Cumulative Evolution in New Caledonian Crow Tool Manufacture." *Proceedings of the Royal Society B* 270 (2003): 867–74.

———. "The Crafting of Hook Tools by Wild New Caledonian Crows." *Proceedings of the Royal Society B (Suppl.)* 271 (2004): S88–90.

Jelbert, Sarah A., Alex H. Taylor, Lucy G. Cheke, Nicola S. Clayton, and Russell D. Gray. "Using the Aesop's Fable Paradigm to Investigate Causal Understanding of Water Displacement by New Caledonian Crows." *PLOS One* (March 26, 2014).

Kenward, Ben, Christian Rutz, Alex A. Weir, and Alex Kacelnik. "Development of Tool Use in New Caledonian Crows: Inherited Action Patterns and Social Influences." *Animal Behaviour* 72 (2006): 1329–43.

Rutz, Christopher, and James J. H. St. Clair. "The Evolutionary Origins and Ecological Context of Tool Use in New Caledonian Crows." *Behavioral Processes* 89 (2012): 153–65.

Stout, Dietrich, and Thierry Chaminade. "Stone Tools, Language and the Brain in Human Evolution." *Philosophical Transactions of the Royal Society B* 367 (2012): 75–87.

Taylor, Alex H., Douglas Elliffe, Gavin R. Hunt, and Russell D. Gray. "Complex Cognition and Behavioral Innovation in New Caledonian Crows." *Proceedings of the Royal Society B* 227 (2010): 2637–43.

Thompson, F. R. "Factors Affecting Nest Predation on Forest Songbirds in North America." *Ibis* 149, issue supplement S2 (November 2007): 98–109.

Tron, François M., Romain Franquet, Trond H. Larsen, and Jean-Jérôme Cassan, eds. *A Rapid Biological Assessment of the Mont Panié Range and Roches de la Ouaième Region, Province Nord, New Caledonia.* Arlington, Va.: Conservation International, 2011.

Wier, Alex X., Jackie Chappell, and Alex Kacelnik. "Shaping of Hooks in New Caledonian Crows." *Science* 297 (August 9, 2002): 981.

PHOTO CREDITS

All images by Andy Comins except for the following:

Page(s)

8 (chimpanzees): Steve Bloom/SteveBloom.com

9 (alligator): Copyright © Dipartimento di Biologia Evoluzionistica, Firenze Italia, reprinted by permission of Taylor & Francis Ltd, www.tandfonline.com on behalf of Dipartimento di Biologia Evoluzionistica, Firenze, Italia

9 (dolphin): Pamela S. Turner

11 (crow on tree limbs): Brian McClatchy

14 (kagu): Dr. Gavin Hunt

15 (tools), 24 (leaves), 25 (tools), 33 (tools): Dr. Gavin Hunt, University of Auckland

30 (squirrels): Can Stock Photo Inc.

38 (crow with pandanus tool): Jennifer Holzhaider, University of Auckland

46 and 47 (Betty the crow), 50 (baby crows and Uék): Alex Kacelnik, Oxford University

49 (crow experiments) Sara Jelbert, University of Auckland

INDEX

Page numbers in **bold** refer to photos and illustrations.

SCIENTISTS IN THE FIELD
Where Science Meets Adventure

Check out these titles to meet more scientists who are out in the field—and contributing every day to our knowledge of the world around us:

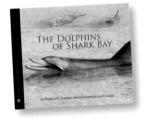

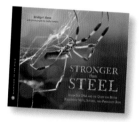

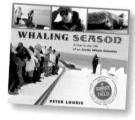

Looking for even more adventure? Craving updates on the work of your favorite scientists, as well as in-depth video footage, audio, photography, and more? Then visit the new Scientists in the Field website!

www.sciencemeetsadventure.com